Grandma MarGie's Tale of God's Creation in 7 Days

Writer: Dr. K. T. Zulkowski

Illustrator: Marina Trapanese

Published by Mz. Kim Productions
4263 Tierra Rejada Rd #151
Moorpark, CA 93021
www.mzkimproductions.com

Zulkowski, Dr. K.T.

Grandma Margie's Tale of The Rain of Faith; I Feel The Rain Drops Falling / Dr. K.T. Zulkowski.

ISBN: 978-1-962106-00-9

Printed in United States of America
First Printing: August 2023
Date of Copyright: July 5, 2023
Cover design by Marina Trapanese
Illustrations by Marina Trapanese
Edited by Joshua Nickel

For permissions, please contact: Mz. Kim Productions

4263 Tierra Rejada Rd #151
Moorpark, CA 93021
www.mzkimproductions.com
mzkimproductions@gmail.com

Dedication Page:

To all the young hearts seeking hope and guidance,

May this book inspire you to embrace the
transformative power of love and faith.

In loving memory of my own Grandma Margie,
Whose stories and wisdom continue to

shape my journey.

And to the future generations,
May you find solace, joy, and endless
possibilities in the pages of this tale.

With gratitude and love,
Dr. K.T. Zulkowski

Author's Note:

Dear readers,

Thank you for choosing "Grandma Margie's Tale Of God's Creation in 7 Days" for your child's reading journey. This book was a labor of love, inspired by my own experiences with my grandmother and my deep appreciation for the beauty of God's creation.

As a renowned author and award-winning filmmaker, I have always been passionate about storytelling and education. Through this book, I aimed to combine these two passions to create an engaging and educational experience for young readers.

I believe that children have an innate sense of wonder and curiosity, and it is our responsibility to nurture and encourage these qualities. By introducing them to the wonders of God's creation through the captivating story of Grandma Margie, Zipporah, and Zion, I hope to inspire a lifelong love for learning and a deep connection to their faith.

I also wanted to emphasize the importance of family bonds and the joy of learning together. Grandma Margie's wisdom and love for her grandchildren are a reflection of the love and guidance that many of us have received from our own grandparents. It is my hope that this book will not only entertain but also strengthen the bonds between generations.

I would like to express my gratitude to the talented illustrator who brought this story to life with their stunning artwork. Their attention to detail and ability to capture the beauty and intricacy of God's creation truly enhances the reading experience.

Lastly, I want to thank you, the readers, for embarking on this journey with us. It is my sincere hope that "Grandma Margie's Tale Of God's Creation in 7 Days" will spark curiosity, nurture a sense of wonder, and instill a deep appreciation for the beauty and complexity of God's creation in the hearts of young readers.

May this book be a source of joy, inspiration, and spiritual growth for you and your family.

With warmest regards,

Dr. K T Zulkowski

Educational Value:

"Grandma Margie's Tale Of God's Creation in 7 Days" offers educational value by teaching children about the importance of nature, the diversity of living creatures, and the significance of rest. It encourages young readers to develop a sense of wonder and appreciation for the world around them, fostering a connection to God's creation.

The book also emphasizes the love and wisdom passed down through generations, as Grandma Margie shares her knowledge and stories with her beloved grandchildren. It highlights the importance of family bonds and the joy of I learning together.

With its engaging narrative, vibrant illustrations, and educational content, "Grandma Margie's Tale Of God's Creation in 7 Days" is a valuable addition to any child's library. It sparks curiosity, nurtures a sense of wonder, and instills a deep appreciation for the beauty and complexity of God's creation.

Overall, this book is an excellent tool for introducing young minds to the wonders of the Bible, fostering a love for learning, and nurturing their spiritual development.

Perfect for children of any age this book is an invaluable resource for parents, grandparents, and educators who wish to introduce young minds to the wonders of the Bible. It fosters a love for reading, a curiosity for learning, and a strong foundation of faith that will accompany children throughout their lives.

Grandma MarGtie's Tale of God's Creation in 7 Days

Writer: Dr. K. T. Zulkowski

Illustrator: Marina Trapanese

Grandma Margie's Tale Of God's Creation in 7 Days

Once upon a time, in a cozy little house, lived Grandma Margie, her granddaughter Zipporah, and grandson Zion. Grandma Margie loved to tell them stories, especially about the wonderful things God had done.

One sunny afternoon Zion asked: *Grandma, can you tell us about how God created the earth?*

Grandma Margie: *Of course, my dear Zion. Let me tell you the incredible story of God's creation.*

Zipporah: *Can we sit in the garden while you tell us, Grandma?*

Grandma Margie: *That sounds like a wonderful idea, Zipporah. Let's go outside and enjoy the sunshine while we learn about God's amazing work.*

1

"*In the beginning, there was nothing but darkness,*"
Grandma Margie began.
"*But God said, 'Let there be light,' and there was light. He separated the light from the darkness, calling the light 'day' and the darkness 'night'.*"

"*And God said, 'Let there be light,' and there was light.*" -

Genesis 1:3

Zion: *Wow, Grandma! God's power is incredible. He can create light out of darkness!*

"On the second day, God created the sky,"
Grandma Margie continued.
"He made it so beautiful, with fluffy clouds and a bright blue color. Then, He separated the waters below from the waters above, creating the seas and the sky."

Zipporah: I love looking up at the sky, Grandma. It's like a big, beautiful painting!

"And God said, 'Let there be a vault between the waters to separate water from water.' So God made the vault and separated the water under the vault from the water above it." ·

Genesis 1:6-7

"Next, on the third day, God made the land and the seas,"
Grandma Margie said.
"He covered the land with green grass, tall trees, and colorful flowers. God made sure that every plant had its own special seed to grow more of its kind."

Zion: *Grandma, I love running through the grass and smelling the flowers. It's all so amazing!*

"And God said, 'Let the land produce vegetation: seed-bearing plants and trees on the land that bear fruit with seed in it, according to their various kinds.' And it was so." -

Genesis 1:11

"On the fourth day, God created the sun, moon, and stars,"
Grandma Margie explained.
"He placed the sun to shine brightly during the day, the moon to glow softly at night, and the stars to twinkle in the sky. They were all so beautiful!"

Zipporah: *Grandma, I love looking up at the night sky and seeing all the stars. It's like a magical show!*

"And God said, 'Let there be lights in the vault of the sky to separate the day from the night, and let them serve as signs to mark sacred times, and days and years.'" -

Genesis 1:14

Now, on the fifth day, God filled the sky and the seas
with amazing creatures,"
Grandma Margie said.
"He made colorful birds that flew high in the sky and
fish that swam gracefully in the deep blue sea. They
were all so unique and wonderful!"

Zipporah: Grandma, I love watching the birds fly and
hearing their beautiful songs. And the fish in the sea
are so graceful!

"And God said, 'Let the water teem with living
creatures, and let birds fly above the earth across the
vault of the sky.'" ·

Genesis 1:20

"On the sixth day, God created all the animals that roam the earth,"
Grandma Margie continued.
"From the tiniest ants to the mighty lions, God made each one special. And then, He created humans, like you and me, in His own image, to take care of His creation."

Zion: Grandma, it's amazing to think that we are made in God's image. We have a special purpose!

"So God created mankind in his own image, in the image of God he created them; male and female he created them." -

Genesis 1:27

"After six days of creating, God looked at everything He had made and saw that it was very good," Grandma Margie said.
"So, on the seventh day, God rested and blessed it as a special day of rest for all of us to enjoy."

Zipporah: *Grandma, I love our special day of rest. It's a time to relax and appreciate all that God has made.*

"By the seventh day, God had finished the work he had been doing; so on the seventh day, he rested from all his work. Then God blessed the seventh day and made it holy because on it he rested from all the work of creating that he had done." -

Genesis 2:2-3

15

Zipporah: *Grandma, that was an amazing story! I can't believe how God created everything so perfectly.*

Zion: *Yeah, Grandma, it's incredible! God's love and creativity are truly remarkable.*

Grandma Margie: *Zipporah and Zion my sweet grandbabies you have listened so well. God's love and creativity are all around us, just waiting to be discovered. Let's continue exploring the wonders of God's creation together.*

Zion: *Yes, Grandma! We want to keep learning and discovering more about God's amazing world.*

Zipporah: *Thank you, Grandma, for sharing this incredible story with us. We love you!*

Grandma Margie: *I love you both too, my dear grandchildren. Let's continue our amazing adventure together, always remembering God's love and creativity.*

The End

www.ingramcontent.com/pod-product-compliance
Lightning Source LLC
Chambersburg PA
CBHW041531120626
46551CB00018B/2651